DEL REY
NEW YORK

Stay safe online. Any website addresses listed in this book are correct at the time of going to print. However, Del Rey is not responsible for content hosted by third parties. Please be aware that online content can be subject to change and websites can contain content that is unsuitable for children. We advise that all children are supervised when using the Internet. This publisher does not have any control over and does not assume any responsibility for author or third-party websites or their content.

ONLINE SAFETY FOR YOUNGER FANS
Spending time online is great fun! Here are a few simple rules to help younger fans stay safe and keep the Internet a great place to spend time:
- Never give out your real name—don't use it as your username.
- Never give out any of your personal details.
- Never tell anybody which school you go to or how old you are.
- Never tell anybody your password except a parent or a guardian.
- Be aware that you must be 13 or over to create an account on many sites. Always check the site policy and ask a parent or guardian for permission before registering.
- Always tell a parent or guardian if something is worrying you.

Originally published in the United States by Del Rey, an imprint of Random House, a division of Penguin Random House LLC, New York.

DEL REY and the HOUSE colophon are registered trademarks of Penguin Random House LLC.

Published in paperback in the United Kingdom by Egmont UK Limited.

ISBN 978-1-9848-2084-6
Ebook ISBN 978-1-9848-2085-3

Printed in China on acid-free paper by C & C Offset

Written by Ed Jefferson

Illustrations by Ryan Marsh

randomhousebooks.com

2 4 6 8 9 7 5 3 1

First US Edition

Design by Maddox Philpot

LET'S BUILD!

LAND OF ZOMBIES

CONTENTS

HELLO FROM SCOUT

Welcome to *Land of Zombies*! I'm Scout, and I'm really excited to be here – there's nothing better than spending a few hours taking down zombies in their various forms. Don't worry, I'll be at your side as you put together all sorts of super-cool builds for these nasties to hang out in.

You'll also meet my friends, the finest comrades anyone could ask for. Sparks loves to build and invent amazing contraptions, while Bear can use his ninja skills to survive almost any situation you can imagine. And Monty? He may not be much use in battle, but, thanks to all that time he spends studying undead mobs in his lab, he has some ace combat tips to share.

In the following pages we're going to help you put together an entire land of amazing zombie-based adventures, and we'll find out what makes these nasty mobs tick along the way.

You'll find it easiest to work on these builds in Creative mode. You may need to seek out different biomes for some of them – there are build ideas here that'll take you from the depths of the ocean to the middle of the desert. Don't worry about replicating the builds block-by-block – get creative and add some personal touches!

Right, let's get going. Sorry, zombies, Scout's coming to visit!

ZOMBIE PROFILES

Another brave adventurer headed into the land of the undead, I see! This is going to be fun! I've had plenty of practice fighting zombies. I've even managed to scribble down a few notes about them in the brief moments when Sparks isn't whispering nervously in my ear about something "coming straight for us"! So let's get to know our opponents, shall we?

HI, I'M SCOUT!

ZOMBIE

The original undead mob, the zombie is usually found lurking in the world's darker places.

DEDICATED FOLLOWERS

If you get too close to a zombie (within 40 blocks), it's game on: They'll lock on to you and try to attack. The bad news is that if you can hear them but not see them, they're probably already coming for you, so keep your weapons ready.

KEEP YOUR DISTANCE

If possible, you want to attack a zombie from a distance so that it can't wave its arms at you. A bow and arrow are ideal for this. If you get into close combat, attack quickly then immediately run backward to avoid its blows.

DAYLIGHT SAVING TIME

If there's one thing a zombie can't stand, it's daylight – if they're caught outside while the sun's up, they'll go up in flames. Be careful, though – I once got too close and singed my eyebrows. And some of them seem to have figured out that wearing a helmet stops them from burning in the sun...

BABY ZOMBIE

These fun-sized zombies will cause you more trouble than you might think.

SPEED DEMONS

The first thing you need to know about these vicious little critters is that they're much faster than regular zombies – and faster than you, too.

Notice the large head.

FIREPROOF

To make things even more interesting, unlike their larger cousins, baby zombies are immune to the effects of daylight. Monty is desperate to capture one to do further research.

This does NOT look comfortable!

TICKET TO RIDE

As if they weren't annoying enough already, baby zombies can also appear as jockeys, riding chickens! So far, I haven't managed to persuade any of my friends to carry me around to test this out as a new combat technique.

TIP !

Some zombies have the ability to pick up dropped items. If they come across tools, weapons, or armor, they will be able to equip and use them, making them more difficult to defeat. Try not to drop anything!

ZOMBIE VARIANTS

Zombies are a lot of fun, but if you want to keep things interesting I'd suggest mixing it up and including a few zombie variants, too. Here's a run-down of what you can expect from the zombie variants.

ZOMBIE VILLAGER

There goes the neighborhood! These villagers might look like they just need a bit of a bath, but they're no less deadly than a regular zombie.

TRAGIC ORIGIN

How does a zombie villager come into existence? Well, when a villager falls to a zombie attack, there's a chance that they'll rise again in this horrible form. Unless you're in Easy mode, that is...

LOOKS ARE SKIN DEEP

They may look different from normal zombies, but all the same rules apply – they'll chase you if you get too close and they burn in daylight.

THE CURE

Monty claims that zombie villagers are not beyond saving – splash them with a potion of weakness, feed them a golden apple, then wait a few minutes – they'll be as good as new.

These robes are extremely dirty

TIP !
Watch out for baby zombie villagers - they're quicker than adults but have the same number of health points.

HUSK

Four out of five zombie spawns in desert biomes will produce a husk.

HUNGRY WORK

Stock up on supplies if you're expecting to battle a lot of these monsters – their attacks will inflict the hunger effect, causing your food bar to drop rapidly.

Someone's been in the sun too long...

SUNNY DISPOSITION

Husks are immune to sunlight. Well, they wouldn't last long in the desert otherwise...

DROWNED

Underwater zombies of the deep, these gruesome guys spawn in darker parts of ocean biomes.

POINTED ATTACKS

Staying out of arms' reach isn't enough with the drowned – they can carry tridents, which they'll throw at you if you're not close enough to attack directly.

BOUND TO THE SEA

The drowned mostly stay underwater, but they have been known to venture out onto the shore at night. Any regular zombie who gets submerged for more than 30 seconds will join the legions of the drowned.

ZOMBIE STATUES

Although not quite as much fun as battling zombies, I've also built a few zombie statues. They will leave visitors in no doubt what this land is all about and also give them a taste of what they're about to experience.

BUILDING MATERIALS

Prismarine blocks and stone bricks are ideal for building these statues. Have fun experimenting with different blocks until you're happy.

CONSTRUCTION

It's easiest to build your statue by starting at the bottom – construct the feet and legs, then work your way upward. You can also save on material by not filling in the insides, which won't be visible anyway.

SCENERY

Try putting your zombie statues into a scene. You could build a giant village hut for them to "attack" and a villager for them to chase. Here we've built a plinth for the zombie to stand on and constructed a sword from cobblestone wall blocks.

HEAD
The zombie's head is a 3 x 3 x 3 block cube of dark prismarine, with a chiseled stone brick block for each eye.

TORSO
The zombie's torso is 3 blocks across, 2 blocks thick and 5 blocks tall. Try combining various stone brick blocks until you're happy with how the torso looks.

ARMS
The arms are 5 x 1 rectangles, attached to the side of the body. The skin is made from dark prismarine and the clothes are made from a variety of stone bricks.

LEGS
The legs should be 4 blocks tall and made from stone brick stairs so they look like they're bending as the zombie moves.

SHOES
Use chiseled stone bricks for the shoes, which are 1 block high at the front and 2 high at the back.

11

MORE STATUE IDEAS

That was fun, right? Well, I have more ideas where those came from. What better way to remember all your glorious victories than with statues of your vanquished foes? Here are a few alternative zombie statue ideas to get you started...

ZOMBIE HEAD

This creepy zombie head makes for a very dramatic sight at night! The head is an 8 x 8 x 8 cube made from various stone blocks. Lava has been placed inside to give it a sinister glow.

Use wall blocks, stairs and stone buttons to create smaller details.

The eyes and mouth are made from lime glass, which allows the lava to shine out.

The combination of stone blocks used to build the head gives the impression it was built long ago.

DROWNED FOUNTAIN

To make this drowned statue you'll
need plenty of prismarine blocks.
The insides are filled with sea lanterns
so that the eyes and mouth glow.
The vines hanging from the sides give it
a derelict feel.

*The water flows out of the
head and cascades down
into an enclosed bowl below.*

*Add some prismarine and
coral blocks in the bowl
area and maybe even a
few sea pickles.*

HUSK SHRINE

Sand is the ideal building material for this
shrine. Have fun combining the different
sand blocks until you're happy.

*The fire on either
side of the husk
reminds us that
husks are immune
to burning in
sunlight.*

*The husk statue is
standing on a red
sandstone plinth –
there's even an altar
made from anvils
and white carpet!*

ZOMBIE MANSION

You know me – being stuck in an enclosed space full of dangerous mobs is my idea of heaven. I built this mansion full of hidden loot, then filled it with the undead to make things interesting. ZOMBIES BEWARE – Scout's coming for you, and I'm bringing a few of my pointiest weapons.

LOVELY LOOT

Leave some hidden surprises in chests to reward those who venture into the mansion. Gold and diamonds are great, but what I really want to discover in the middle of a zombie fight is a shiny new weapon. That's actually how I found Dragon Slasher, one of my trustiest blades!

ABANDONED ATMOSPHERE

Cobwebs and vines will add to the mansion's creepy, run-down feel – they'll slow any explorers down a bit, but with my awesome combat skills it's only fair to the poor zombies, right?

DEAD ENDS

Make sure any reluctant warriors (mentioning no names) won't just run straight out the other side – add some unexpected dead ends. Sure, you might find yourself pinned down by a horde of zombies, but that's what all these weapons are for.

LIGHTS OUT

Battle's no fun if you know what to expect, so make sure some areas of the mansion are hidden in darkness. Block up windows, take out torches – anything to create more shadows for mobs to lurk in! It might get a bit scary for Sparks, but she knows I've got her back.

MUSIC TO WHACK THINGS TO

The moans of the zombies are a pretty good soundtrack to get you in the battling mood, but a jukebox or three never hurts. I like the disc "ward" – it's got spooky bits to suit a zombie mansion, but you can smash mob heads in time with that funky beat.

SECRET DUNGEON

Once you've customized your mansion just the way you like it, why not add another fun challenge and build a secret dungeon full of even more nasty mobs to defeat? Let's take a look at how to make it really, really spooky.

GET THE DUNGEON LOOK

Stairs lead down to your mansion's gloomy cellar – build the walls out of cobblestone, lit with torches (but not too many!) and perhaps leave a few mob heads around the place as a reminder of the grisly fate of those who didn't make it out of here.

Redstone torches cast a dimmer glow.

CORRIDOR OF DARKNESS

On one side of your dungeon, carve out a long corridor, stretching around to a dead end. Add a spawner at the end of the corridor.

Listen for the sound of rattling bones here!

IMPRISONED FOR GOOD REASON

Construct some stone cells with sturdy iron doors, then trap zombies inside (they can't break through iron). Woe betide anyone who tries a prison break down here!

Moss stone gives a damp vibe.

The doors are controlled by a lever.

SECRET ENTRANCE

Hide the entrance to the dungeon behind a painting. To do this you'll need to carve out a 2-block-high doorway. Place signs on each side of the doorway, on the top and bottom block. You'll then be able to place a painting over the top, hiding the entrance, but allowing visitors to pass through.

Libraries often have secret entrances.

TIP !

There are several different sizes of painting - keep experimenting until you're happy with your secret entrance.

DEFEND THE VILLAGE

Are zombies attacking your local village? Villagers at their wits' end? Let me show you how to help them survive any zombie attack and make those undead monsters wish they'd stayed at home. Just keep quiet until we've finished, so they don't hear us...

RAISE THE DOORS
Zombies can break down doors, but only if they're standing on the same level. Moving the building doors 1 block up will keep them out. Don't worry, the villagers will still be able to use them!

BLOCK THE VILLAGERS IN
Once all your villagers are indoors, you can pen them into the area. Fence gates are ideal, as you can open them but zombies and villagers can't. This should only be a temporary measure while you install better defenses.

LET THERE BE LIGHT
Zombies can only spawn in darkness, so place torches or glowstone blocks around the village. This will prevent any nasty surprises when the sun goes down.

SECURE ENTRANCE

Zombies can't break down iron doors, so to make a secure village entrance, place iron doors in the wall, with levers or buttons on either side to control them. Your villagers won't be able to get past the doors, but they're safer in here anyway. Don't use pressure plates, as the doors will open if zombies step on them.

FENCE THEM OUT

Build a stone wall all the way around the village. Make it at least 3 blocks high to keep out any wandering zombies who stumble into the area and decide they enjoy feasting on the villagers.

WE'RE READY FOR THEM NOW!

GOLEMS

Some people say it's "cheating" to have something else fight your battles for you, but as far as I'm concerned it's just common sense. Golems are an ideal defensive measure for a village when you just can't be around.

IRON GOLEMS

Iron golems are a key part of a village's defense – they'll spawn automatically in any village with 10 villagers and 21 wooden doors.

SNOW GOLEMS

Snow golems aren't as useful for defense because their attacks won't actually hurt zombies, but they will slow them down. Also, because they can attack from a distance you can put them up in a tower out of harm's way.

To build an iron golem, assemble 4 iron blocks in a T-shape, then place a pumpkin or jack o'lantern on top.

Iron golems are an extremely effective defense – when they attack a mob it'll go flying through the air.

Watch out – if you attack a villager the iron golem will come after you!

To build a snow golem, stack 2 blocks of snow and top with a pumpkin or jack o'lantern.

Build 3 or more snow golems to ensure they'll throw enough snowballs to keep the zombies away.

If you want your snow golems to look a bit friendlier (and less pumpkin-y) you can use shears to remove their pumpkins.

WRECKED CONTAINER SHIP

Ah, life under the sea – there's so much to discover! Like this wrecked container ship, which has sunk to the sea floor and split in two. And what will you find inside? Plenty of loot for any aquatic adventurers, and plenty of drowned to battle, too.

CONTAINERS

Build a 4 x 4 x 10 solid container using a colored concrete of your choice. Use different colors of concrete to build multiple containers along the deck, then build another layer of containers on top. Avoid stacking containers of the same color next to each other or they won't look like separate units.

UNDERWATER DECORATION

Seagrass and coral can be placed around the wreck to give the impression that the ship has been abandoned beneath the waves for countless years. You could also cover part of your deck in horrible green slime blocks – I'm sure that'll make the drowned feel at home!

UPPER DECKS

Use gray concrete to build a deck 1 block below the top of the hull so there's a small wall running around the edge. At the back of the deck, use white concrete to build a tower 10 blocks high, 20 blocks across the deck and 10 blocks long – this will become the bridge and crew compartments.

HULL

The hull of the ship split in two and we're just going to build the back half. Use red concrete to build the hull. As you build up, extend the hull by 1 block every 3 or 4 blocks so the ship is wider at the top than at the base. You want the ship to be about 60 blocks long and 30 blocks wide at the top.

INVITE THE DROWNED

If you want to attract some drowned to haunt your shipwreck, place a few turtle eggs on the deck. Like other zombies, drowned seek them out so they can trample them. Another good reason to take them out!

CREW COMPARTMENTS

Now you've got the outside of the wreck looking great, it's time to give the interior a bit more detail. We'll start with the bridge and other compartments inside the white tower you built on the deck. I wonder what the crew left behind?

SHIP CONTROLS

Ships are complex vehicles that require lots of controls. Place blocks of green and red concrete in item frames, then position them around the bridge on top of wood planks. Add a few levers for good measure.

SLEEPING QUARTERS

The ship's crew would have needed somewhere to sleep. Create sleeping quarters by placing beds on the deck with chests surrounding them. You could also place the odd block of carpet on the concrete floor to give it a homey feel.

WINDOW

Dig out a 2-block-high space running along the front of the bridge and replace it with glass panes or blocks. Once you've done this you can use sponge blocks in the bridge to remove the water.

WHEEL

In the center of the window make a 2-block-high column of wood planks. Then, facing the window, attach another block of planks to the back of the top block. Place levers on the sides, top and bottom of this block and set each to the same position – now you've got a ship's steering wheel!

TOP OF THE SHIP

Start by building a floor of gray concrete halfway up the tower. Place a trapdoor in one corner and run a ladder on the wall up to it. This is how you'll access the bridge from the lower decks.

MOOD LIGHTING

Place a few sea lanterns, then top and surround the sides of each one with wood slabs. This gives you just enough light to see, but is gloomy enough that you never know what might creep up on you.

THE HOLD

This room, deep within the ship, is where the most valuable cargo would have been stored. Unfortunately, the drowned got here first and are marauding around the bowels of the wreck. You'll have to fight them off before you can snag the loot.

CONTAINER MAZE

Use colored concrete to build more containers like the ones on deck. This way, you can block off parts of the decks so it's harder to navigate and avoid any drowned who've found their way in here.

SEABED

On the lower deck, add a few blocks of dirt in some areas where the seabed has broken through the hull. You can also scatter a few blocks of gray concrete underneath the hole where the ceiling collapsed.

BREATHING ROOM

Create a breathing room where adventurers can catch their breath.

SUNKEN TREASURE

Replace 1 block within some of the containers with a chest and fill it with valuable loot - that's what the ship must have been carrying! Put different items in each container's chest - one could be full of weaponry, one full of food, and so on. One could even be full of gold - treasure isn't just for pirates!

DOUBLE DECKER

Split the interior of the hull in two with a 1-block-high floor of gray concrete. Leave a 10-block-wide hole in the middle, so it seems like the deck collapsed when the ship hit the sea floor! Use sponge to clear the interior of water.

ZOMBIE ARENA

I love fighting zombies: Who doesn't? But hunting them down? Yawn! This zombie arena will get the battle started whenever YOU feel like it. Last one in is a wimp!

WALLS
Make a ring of cobblestone blocks, leaving a space of at least 50 blocks in the middle. Build up the ring with walls that are at least 4 blocks high and 1 block thick to keep the zombies contained.

SEATING
To complete the arena, top out the ring with stepped tiers of blocks to act as seats.

GATES
To access the arena, build an entrance using lever-controlled iron doors. That way, the zombies can't escape.

EEK!

ROOF

If you want to encourage zombie combat during the day, you'll need to add a roof so the monsters aren't burned up in the sun. Well, unless an endlessly refillable pit of burning zombies is your idea of fun...

VIEWING PLATFORM

As well as providing the best views of the action, this is where you'll control the release of zombies and other mobs into the arena.

GOLEMS

If you don't want to get your hands dirty (or you're too much of a scaredy-cat to enter the arena yourself), you can always stage some zombie vs. golem battles. Iron golems will be most effective – place a pumpkin on top of 4 iron blocks arranged in a T-shape to make one.

ENTER THE ZOMBIES

Now you've built your arena, you're going to need some zombies. You could try opening the doors and waiting, or you could simply press a button on my handy zombie dispenser for an instant battle!

1 Place 3 blocks on the ground at the side of the arena, then 3 dispensers filled with zombie spawn eggs on top.

2 Add a solid block of redstone to power the dispensers, with redstone dust to each side as shown.

3 Add a U-shape of blocks 2 blocks above the redstone block, and place a redstone torch as shown.

4 Place a sticky piston facing down so that it touches the redstone block when extended. Add redstone dust in a circle as shown.

7 Attach 2 more blocks to the last block you placed, with a button on top. Press the button to release the zombies!

6 Add 1 more block with redstone dust. Add a redstone torch to the side of the block you just placed. This forms the downward power transfer.

5 Add 2 more blocks above the sticky piston, with redstone dust on top. Now place a redstone torch on the side of the block at the back, as shown.

GRAVEYARD

This zombie-filled graveyard is an opportunity to show off your awesome design skills as well as your bravery. Have fun creating a suitably spooky setting, then launch yourself into battle alongside your friends!

WALL

Use a mixture of cobblestone and moss stone blocks to build a wall around the outside of the graveyard. You can also use iron bars to create railings on top of the wall.

I WAS BORN FOR THIS!

TALL GRASS

Make your graveyard seem overgrown with tall or double tall grass. You can use bone meal on grass to make it grow taller. Place vines and cobwebs on buildings and memorials. Add trees and dead bushes, too.

GRAVES

To make a simple gravestone, place several stairs on top of each other. Stone brick stairs and quartz stairs look good. You can also place a row of 2-3 blocks of dirt behind them to mark out the grave. If you're looking for a really creepy effect, use soul sand instead.

MEMORIALS

Give your graveyard a bit of variety: 2 stairs placed back-to-back make another simple gravestone. You could also get creative with mob heads and make small sculptures to stand guard over the graves.

PATHS

Run paths from the entrance of your graveyard past each row of graves. They can also run up to your crypt or any other memorials so that you'll always have easy access.

THE CRYPT

Anyone who's truly explored the Land of the Undead will tell you that the real experience is to be found under the ground – which is why every good graveyard needs a crypt. Here are some tips to make it look super creepy.

 1 Don't worry about the crypt interior yet – build the outside to look really cool and spooky and make sure you've got space for some stairs. Most of the interior will be below ground so you'll be able to dig it out and make it as large as you like.

2 A door made of dark oak provides the right sort of look – iron doors with a suitable control (a lever or button) also work.

3 Place signs near the entrance listing some of the unfortunate souls to be found within. Perhaps you could use the names of any friends who've fallen in battle to zombies lately.

Every good crypt needs a few gruesome gargoyles. Pick a few spots on the roof – corners are good – and construct gargoyles by placing a mob head on the side of a slab block. Zombie heads work well for this or, if you want something really menacing, try a dragon head.

 For an eerie effect, use glowing blocks behind glass panes to make windows in the crypt walls. Glowstone works really well for this – the otherworldly glow will make your crypt truly haunting.

INSIDE THE CRYPT

Stuck underground with the undead about to feast on you? Your only way out blocked by zombies? Sounds like my kind of party! These crypt interiors will add a whole other level to your graveyard – literally.

THE BASICS

As you dig out your crypt, reinforce everything with stone and add stone pillars/columns for supports.

COFFINS

Dig 2-block-long holes in the floor and place 2 trapdoors over the top to give the effect of coffins. You could place a zombie spawner inside and leave the trapdoors open so zombies emerge to terrorize visitors.

BANNERS

To complete your decorations, hang some banners around the walls – this green banner works particularly well with the zombie theme. A healthy sprinkling of cobwebs will finish things off nicely.

SKELETON HEADS

To make your crypt truly chilling, dig out blocks in the wall and fill them with skeleton heads, then place a few on the floor for good measure.

ZOMBIE SIEGE

It's all very well hunting zombies in the wild, but this zombie siege chamber will really test your skills. How many zombies can you release into the chamber before you're totally overpowered? Let's find out!

THE SPAWNING CHAMBER

The spawning chamber lies just out of sight, behind these zombies. Choose how many zombies to spawn depending on how brave you're feeling, then activate the dispensers and open the door using the levers at the other end of the corridor (see page 40 for a tutorial). Make sure the chamber is at least 5 blocks deep so there's room for a zombie horde.

THE SIEGE CORRIDOR

The corridor is 30 blocks long and designed to look like a mountain valley, with a fort at one end and the spawning room at the other. The stone walls have been decorated with vines and the floor is made from grass and dirt blocks.

ROOM WITH A VIEW
Build the walls out of stone bricks, with a viewing platform on top of the keep and along each side of the corridor. That way, you can invite spectators to watch the fun!

THE FINISH LINE
If any zombies reach the red finish line at the end of the corridor, you've lost the siege. A trip wire connected to note blocks will let you know when this happens.

TIP

Stock up on wooden trapdoors - placing them between you and the zombie hordes will buy you some time.

REDSTONE MECHANICS

What good is a zombie siege without any zombies, eh? Let's create some clever redstone circuits to power the zombie dispensers, as well as a release mechanism, and get this party started!

CONTROL ROOM

This lies just inside the fortress. The lever on the right controls the dispensers. The lever on the left controls the doors that release the zombies at the other end of the corridor.

Build a castle gate out of spruce trapdoors.

CLOCK CIRCUIT

The clock circuit beneath the control room provides a pulse signal to the dispensers. When you pull the lever, the dispensers start producing zombies, and they'll stop when you pull the lever again.

Use repeaters to relay power to the spawn room.

You'll need an odd number of torches.

SPAWNING CHAMBER

This lies at the opposite end of the corridor from the control room. Place dispensers in the spawning chamber and power them with redstone torches. The doors are powered by the repeaters at each side.

Obsidian is always a nice choice for that spooky look.

Run one circuit down into a channel so it's separate from the other.

POWER TRANSFER

Power is transferred up to the doors on either side via the redstone as shown. The torches at the back transfer power up to the dispensers. Make sure the redstone dust wires don't cross or your circuits will get tangled up!

The redstone channels should be 2 blocks deep.

THE FINISH LINE

Let's take a closer look at the finish line at the end of the corridor. There's a trip wire built into it to let you know when a zombie has made it through to the end of the chamber, so you know when you've lost. Follow these steps to set it up.

1 Mark out the finish line by replacing the floor with a row of colorful blocks. Red concrete works well for this, but you can use anything that contrasts with the rest of the floor.

2 Place trip wire hooks at either side of the finish line. Make a hole in the corridor wall on both sides and place the hooks in the gaps to make sure your trip wire covers the entire corridor.

3 Now lay down string on top of your row of colorful blocks until the trip wire hooks are connected. You should now have a working trip wire.

To ensure your zombies keep heading in the right direction, you can place villagers or turtle eggs at the end of the corridor to entice them. This only works if your corridor is less than 40 blocks long; otherwise the zombies won't notice them.

 Place note blocks on top of the blocks that the trip wire is attached to and select suitable notes. Now when any zombies cross the line, a sound will play.

WILD WEST ZOMBIES

Well, this doesn't look good – husks have been roaming the desert and have chased away the inhabitants of this Wild West town. This would never have happened if I'd been around to help! Here's how to build a convincingly monster-ravaged frontier town to have some fun in.

TOWN MOBS

The townspeople are gone, but they've left a few of their animals. Spawn some chickens to wander around the town, and cows and horses in fenced-off areas. Who knows, the horses may even come in handy when you're fighting off husks!

HUSK DEFENSES

The townspeople didn't give up without a fight! Try using hay bales to make small fortifications at regular intervals along the main street and just outside the town. Place them in a row 2-5 blocks long and 1-2 blocks high.

TOWN BOUNDARY

Run a wooden fence around the boundary where you're going to build your town. For the entrance, leave a 5-block-wide gap. At either side of the gap, stack 5 fence blocks on top of each other, then connect the two sides with some more fences at the top.

DESERT BUILDING MATERIALS

Wood is the key building material for your town. Make your designs stand out by using birch, spruce and dark oak on different parts of the houses and other buildings in your town. Wooden slabs and fences also come in handy for adding detail.

RED ROADS

Run paths from your town entrance to each building using coarse dirt, red sand, and grass path blocks. Here we've created a 5-block-wide "main street" running through the center of the town, with single-block-wide paths running off it to the buildings.

FRONTIER BUILDINGS

Great, you've got the basic look and layout of your Wild West town sorted! Now you can get cracking on the details. Here are a few build ideas to get you started. We're going to build a Wild West town so awesome that even your cowardly friends will happily risk getting attacked by husks to have a look around!

SHERIFF'S OFFICE

Turn one of the buildings into a sheriff's office by building a row of jail cells inside using iron bars. You could even spawn some husks inside the cells to provide some moaning, undead prisoners. An item frame with a mob head inside makes for a great "wanted" poster.

THE GENERAL STORE

Line the walls of this building with shelves – rows of wooden planks alternating with chests. Fill up each chest with a different item you might need for mining and fighting husks. Place signs on the front of each chest, labeled with the contents, so shoppers can find what they need.

TOWN SALOON

No frontier town is complete without a saloon. Place a pair of fence gates in the doorway to create a saloon door. To create a bar, place a row of planks a block away from the back wall, and hang item frames on the wall behind it with glass bottles and potions inside.

WATER TOWER

Use a combination of moss stone, stone wall and wooden fence blocks to build the legs of your water tower – place them in each corner of a 5 x 5 square. Extend the legs up for about 10 blocks, then build a tank on top using wood planks before filling it with water. Add a small ledge around the base of the tank using wood slabs. Run an access ladder up one side and it can double as a watch tower! Finally, use buttons and trapdoors to add decorative detail.

TIP !

To give unwary visitors a shock, add a trapdoor to the bottom of the tank then use some drowned spawn eggs in the water. Anyone opening that door will unleash a whole new kind of undead on this poor town. Hasn't it suffered enough?

ABANDONED GOLD MINE

Looks like this gold mine must have been abandoned when the townspeople were chased away by the husks. I wonder if there's anything interesting inside it...I'll investigate while you build your Old West–style mineshaft entrance!

1 If there are no suitable hillsides or mountainsides near your town, build the tunnel out of the ground using stone blocks, then cover it in a layer of sand blocks. This will give the effect of a mineshaft poking out of the ground.

2 Stack some blocks near the mine-cart tracks to look like they have just come up from, or are on their way down to the mine. We've used various ores and added in a few blocks of TNT.

3 This isn't just any mine tunnel – something terrible has happened here! Place a few skeleton heads near the entrance to give visitors the sense that danger is lurking within.

4 Use stripped dark oak wood to make three "beams" to outline the mine's entrance. Make sure the wood that makes up each beam is oriented the same way so it looks like one solid block. Place a torch on either side to mark the entrance once it's built.

5 This was previously a working mine, so run tracks of rail from the entrance into the tunnel. Place at least one mine cart on a piece of the track outside. Who knows, they may come in handy for exploring the mine!

UNDEAD CITY

This entire city has been abandoned and left to the zombies – you're going to need an exceptional team by your side to help you battle your way out of this one! Let's take a look at how to construct an undead city.

GRID SYSTEM

Create roads at right angles to one another, in a grid system, with squares of land in between for the buildings. Lay out 5-block-wide roads using black concrete. Each square of land is around 20 x 20 blocks, with a 1-block-wide pavement of stone between the building and the road.

BUILDING MATERIALS

When putting your buildings together, choose blocks that will give your designs an urban feel – concrete, bricks, stone bricks, and glass are going to be used a lot here. Cracked and mossy stone bricks will also help to make your city feel abandoned.

ROAD DESIGN

To add the finishing touches, replace the middle row of blocks in each road with white concrete to create two lanes. To make your city feel even more derelict you can also replace a few blocks of each road with grass, as if the concrete has worn away over time.

STREET DETAIL

Streets looking a little bare? Let's add some streetlights! Make the posts out of stacked iron bars and place a light-emitting block like a sea lantern on the top. Add some street furniture as well – stairs with trapdoors on the side make a great bench.

PARK LIFE

Once the heart of the city, at night this park is overrun by the undead. Cover the block in grass, close it off with iron bars, but leave an entrance in the center of each side. Use bonemeal on the grass to create tall grass and make it seem overgrown.

SKYSCRAPER

A boring old office block? Why would you want to go there? Because it's full of zombies, of course! Let's walk through the build of one floor to get you started, then you can let your imagination run wild with the rest. I wonder what happens when you push a zombie down an elevator shaft...

1 Create desks by placing rows of wood planks. If you want to give some of them computers, place quartz stairs on top and place a painting against it to look like a screen. Place sea lanterns in the ceiling to create fluorescent office lighting.

TIP **!**

A monochrome color scheme works well for an office - try using black, white, and gray blocks to create the interior. Avoid anything too bright.

2 Each floor has a base of iron blocks, with walls of glass that are 3 blocks high. Here we've used carpet on the iron blocks but missed the occasional square to give it that run-down look. You could also leave a few gaps in the glass windows, where they've been smashed by flailing zombies.

3 Near the center of each floor, build a 3 x 3 concrete box that spans from floor to ceiling, with an open space in one side – this will form the elevator shaft that links each floor. Looks like this elevator has been broken for a long time, so place a ladder running all the way up the building, next to the opening – this is how adventurers will move from floor to floor.

4 Once you're finished with this floor, repeat the basic design on top of it, but feel free to add some variety to encourage explorers to go all the way to the top. Maybe you could put something extra special on the roof, like a swimming pool full of drowned!

MORE CITY BUILD IDEAS

I like to fill my city with lots of different builds. That way, it has plenty of variety and provides me with a number of places to practice my latest combat techniques. Here are a few ideas and tips to get you going. I can't wait to disappear into the shadows of whatever you create!

SHOPPING MALL

Once packed full of shoppers, this shopping center is now home to packs of zombies seeking shelter from the sun.

Divide up the interior into several shops and use different colors of concrete for the walls.

Place signs or item frames by the entrance to each shop and use them to show what each shop sold before the zombies moved in.

Use white concrete for the floors and ceilings.

TIP !

Decorate the exterior of your shopping mall using leaf blocks and the occasional dead bush. This will give it the same overgrown, abandoned vibe as the rest of the town. Some of the leaf blocks could even cover the windows.

Drop a chest in the back of each shop and fill it with different items—you could have a clothes shop full of armor, one stocked with food, and another with tools and weapons.

CINEMA

If this cinema is still screening any films, they must be something that appeals to the city's new zombie population...

Construct tiers for the seats by building 2-block-wide "steps" out of black concrete. Place acacia stairs and trapdoors along the back row of each tier to create seats.

Build a screen out of white concrete on the wall facing the seats.

FOUNTAIN

Why not add a fountain for the zombie residents to enjoy? Let's hope they don't get drowned...

Build a perimeter wall out of bricks to mark out the area.

Replace the ground inside the square with a mix of stone and andesite blocks.

Arrange blocks of quartz in a pillar in the center.

Use a water bucket on the top of the quartz pillar to create your fountain.

Add a few decorative details, like a tent made from wool and a campfire made from netherrack.

TOP SECRET LAB

At last, it's the zombie testing lab Monty's always dreamed of! It's ideal for collecting specimens and trying out a few experiments on them, but it would also be a lot of fun if we let them out...

A SOLID FOUNDATION

Build the walls, floors, and ceiling from quartz blocks to give your lab a clean white look. Set sea lanterns into the ceiling at regular intervals to provide lighting across the lab.

SPECIMEN CHAMBERS

To aid you with your studies, pick a wall and build chambers for live specimens that you've captured: dig out a series of 2-block-high, 1-block-wide, and 2-block-deep chambers, then spawn a different mob into the back of each (e.g., one of each kind of zombie). Once you've spawned each one, immediately block the entrance with glass.

POTION WALL

Place a row of dispensers a block apart and fill each with a different kind of potion. Next, hollow out a 2-block-deep space behind each dispenser, and top each dispenser with a column of glass. Fill the gap behind each column with water, dyed to match the color of the potion. Finally, place a button next to each dispenser, and your potion wall is complete.

WORKBENCH

Make sure your lab is properly equipped with all the crafting equipment you might need. Include a brewing stand, cauldron, anvil, furnace, crafting table, and enchantment table.

EXPERIMENTAL CHAMBER

Here comes the really cool part – this chamber will let you demonstrate how to create zombie villagers. This is much safer for Monty than letting him try to witness it in the wild. I wonder if he'll let me open the chamber, though...

1 First, build the base of your chamber using colorful concrete blocks – this one is 5 x 9 blocks. At one end this will connect to buttons and levers, while at the other it will connect to your dispensers.

2 Place a redstone torch and repeater, then add redstone dust as shown. This pattern forms 3 separate circuits, which transfer power from the front to the back of the chamber.

3 Place 2 more concrete blocks with redstone dust on top as shown. Place another 3 concrete blocks, then place 2 buttons and a lever on top of these. Add several more concrete blocks to cover the circuit at the front and act as a hazard strip.

6 Build up the walls with more iron blocks and glass. Add an iron door to the front and 3 dispensers and a redstone torch to the back. Add lava buckets to the top dispenser (to get rid of the zombies once you've finished your experiment), then zombie spawn eggs and villager eggs to the other two. When the zombies attack the villagers, they'll turn them into zombie villagers.

5 Move to the back of the chamber and add another layer of iron blocks (we've flipped the image here so you can see the back clearly). Add some glass along the sides as shown. Place 2 repeaters and a torch at the back as well – these will power the dispensers.

4 Add iron and quartz blocks as shown. This will be the floor of the chamber. Add 4 sea lanterns to light it up. Extend the redstone circuit at the back.

DE-ZOMBIFICATION CHAMBER

Has your local village been inflicted with a bout of zombie-ism? Don't worry! Install this chamber in your lab, and you'll be able to safely cure zombie villagers of their condition. You'll be hailed as a hero!

1 The chamber should be 3 x 3 x 3 blocks – you want to leave a space 2 blocks high and 1 block long and across. Leave a 2-block-high, 1-block-wide opening in the front, and a single block opening in the center of each side, a block above the ground.

2 Place a dispenser pointing inward, and load the dispenser up with splash potions of weakness. This is the first component of your zombie cure. Add a button on the block next to the dispenser – pressing it will launch the potion at whatever's in the chamber.

3 Place a chest next to the chamber opening and fill it with golden apples. You'll need to feed one to the zombie villager through the opening in the chamber. The transformation takes a few minutes.

4 You don't want your uncured zombie villager wandering around the lab, so place an iron trapdoor in the front opening, controlled by a lever on one side. Once cured, you can hit the lever to let the villager out.

5 Display a hideous zombie villager in a glass pod at the side of the de-zombification chamber, to show everyone exactly what the chamber is for.

 5

TIP !

If you want to try the chamber without herding a zombie into it, place a second dispenser underneath the first, and fill with zombie villager spawn eggs. Add another button and you're all set!

BYE FOR NOW

Amazing work. Best Land of Zombies EVER, if you ask me. You should sell tickets! But don't stop there, I'm sure you'll be able to think of more builds to make it even more dangerous.

Anyway, I think I've just picked up the trail of some nasty mobs lurking somewhere around here, so I'd better go and show them why you never mess with Scout.

I'm sure we'll have some brilliant new things to create together soon, but until then, keep your builds awesome and your weapons close!

STAY IN THE KNOW!